AF507518

Poetic Freedom

BORN A CAGED BIRD

Mario Finesse Wright

Poetic Freedom: Born a Caged Bird
Influential Books

Mario F. Wright
P.O Box 20696
New York, NY 10021

Email: mariofwright@gmail.com
Instagram: @Influentialfinesse

*This book is dedicated to everyone in the struggle,
the many struggles of this beautiful life.*

MOTHERLESS CHILD

Back in 1988...

Momma pushed me out, then she bounced, how a kid like that supposed to amount?
Daddy Heroic, nah Daddy Heroin, so the streets is what I found.
How come you didn't tell me about the traps society set for us?
That if I didn't die young, a cell is where I'll end up.
Jail, I grew up thinking that's somewhere we all had to go.
Your smart Pop, was your mind so polluted that you didn't know?
If my mother is a prostitute, how am I ever supposed to respect a woman?
Then Grandma came around, thank God I met that woman.
Wassup Pimping? I know you wanted me to pick up your profession.
A confession, I didn't like the way it looked, I rather pick up a weapon.
So, I hit the streets, in my twisted mind, I thought that was where I would find love.
Just end up finding brothers that was more messed up than I was.
I don't want your pity, just recollecting, taking it back to the gritty.
I'm nobody's victim and I don't want no misdirection.
Those my O.G.'s, love and respect them.
They were this way before I was conceived and if they weren't,
I would never be
so gladly I accept them.
Just a little story, let you know no matter your curse.

There's always someone's story that a end up being worse.
Overcome it, don't let it break you down.
Take your time young kings and queens and one day you'll come around.

WISE GARDENERS

My parents were in the garden
looking for the coca leaf
while there
they planted a seed
smart they were
and came up with me

YOU BELONG TO THE CITY

Sidiq's Prelude

"I'm a tell you a story Son, on how I know you was
destined to be something special and a problem for
this world. You were around three, four years old, yet
already a grown man advanced like this wasn't your
first go around. I brought you along to New York
City to handle some business. This was the early 90's
New York before Giuliani shut everything down, it
was off the hook. I held your hand as we got off at
Port Authority, the most crowded station I've ever set
foot in. Anyhow, 42nd and 8th was its usual drug
dealers, pimps, hoes, addicts, everyone hustling,
everything right there in front of you. Surely this
wasn't a place to bring a child. I would have expected
you to be scared or nervous in the crowd of all the
people with the commotion and the noise, but I was
the one shocked when I looked down at your face.
Your eyes were lit up like a kid on his best
Christmas... I was taken aback on how comfortable
you looked taking it all in... At that point, I seen what
I created. Though I may have thought of setting a
better example, by the look I seen in your eyes, I
knew it was too late. It was at that moment that I
came to the conclusion that, you belong to the city."

What was it that caused that spark in my young eyes?
What normally could have caused the sound of a
child's cries.
Was it the millions of pieces of broken glass and gum
stains stuck on the sidewalk,

or the smooth man with the grin and how his hand
would spin while he fast talked?
What was it that rooted my expression,
the looks on their faces, full of intoxication,
mixed with the joy and the hurt,
the variety of legs that moved in strange directions,
or the way her hips swayed in front of me,
the pleasures in a skirt?
Was it the smell of the hamburger spot, along with
the couple smoking pot,
mixed with the antifreeze from the car that soaked the
ground when it dropped?
I seen many different stores and different color signs,
the big ones that read 'Peep Show'.
And all the different colors of all these different cool
looking people,
the brown ones like my Daddy, the ones white like
my Mommy,
did I see the struggle, the hustle, the grimy?
Was this my training day, unbeknownst to me,
my early days as a rookie?
The lady that pinched my cheek said, "He's so cute,"
as she handed over a fortune cookie.
She turned and left out the Chinese food store, I
smiled and said, "Sucker!"
Did I know she was a whore,
the ones that dressed just like my mother?
I was busy observing, couldn't talk but if I did, no one
could hear me though,
all the car's noises, and the blended voices
and the kid walking, listening to his stereo.
Was it the blind feel of crime that was right before
my eyes,
the connection, the vibes when two men clapped
hands that I would later come to prize?
Was that a formal greeting or a drug deal in disguise?

Was it the love, or the lies,
the jewels, the pearls,
the cops, the quarrels,
the bouts, the stress,
the shouts, the sex,
was it because I was named Finesse, born into this
mess?
I've grown to learn
not to ignore
that I love to absorb
all people, all things, and all of life
but this was the first presented to me in my young
eyesight.
So, no matter what it was, whether right or wrong,
the streets,
the struggle,
the ghetto,
the hustle,
the City,
was where I belonged.

THE THREE WISE MONKEYS

I remember the first time we went to the youth house,
eleven years old on the roof house. Looking down
smashing their car windows chanting "fuck the
police!" until they came running towards us, arresting
us. Us against them, right? Who was I kidding? Or
the time I got caught and you didn't, police had me on
my grandmother's porch. I seen you bend the corner
tapping the 'shhhhh!' hand signal against your lips.
Youngins, we knew the rules then, we know the rules
now. How the three of us stuck together so long, I
seen brothers admire us for that in our town. Like the
LOX of our block, loyalty and love? But the LOX
never broke up, so you spat in everybody's face when
you choked up. Spat in my face, hold up! I always did
good, bringing you along, taking you out of the hood.
Helped you with a place to stay, hustling- I paved a
way. Assisted you on the run, money on your books,
even paid for the lawyer. Funny-money, how your
own pop didn't want to help with the lawyer. Wifey
knew what's up, when she needed help the bros was
who she called. Whole time you planned to do it; she
knew all along. How could you help them people
against your own people? To sing that song, the
music of evil. Fed beef is rare in our hood, so when
they snatched the bros, you were thinking, 'They're
done up anyway!' Nah you know me, I'm a do my
time, come home and come up anyway. This poem I
may never deposit, might lock it away somewhere in
a closet. Don't think I write this because I'm hurt or
with no ill will. That's something you have to live
with kid. This for others on that bid, across I came, so
many felt the same. You know how I relate, I'm a
find a way to help with their pain. To help and serve

my people was always my aim. Little by little, I'm achieving.

I've learned there are two types of people in this world: one that will stand and die for what he believes in, the other, who lacks morals and integrity. We choose our destiny. I realized you are nothing like me and Milly. Sent you out to Vegas, trusted you in Hollywood, I was silly.

If we do better, what they're trying to do to us is stoppable. So, I'm a make it as clear as possible… I can never help the ones oppressing, destroying, and killing us. That's for the future ones. Before you make that decision you may not even understand, just hush!

NIGHTMARE

I don't want to be evil but in order to be equal
to people, I have to.
Because it a grab you,
in the dark.
It's dark where I been, yeah, it's dark there.
Scared of the dark?
I don't know because I'm used to it.
Since I was born impotent, fear is an emotion
I learned to face head on.
Dead wrong, until fear turns into "he's strong!"
Now if I wake up, it's to a drug bust.
Vengeful thoughts are dreading,
and disrespectful-excessive lust
kills my chances of a wedding.
Broken trust.
I don't know why gunfights excite the night,
until I die.
I can't help what goes on inside.
I tried...
Then I cried.
I dream in doubt.
Revenge in my sleep, fighting my best friend.
And I creep in sin,
with disloyal lovers.
Addicted mothers.
Fathers stealing.
Drug dealing-drug healing.
Bad company.
Children hungry.
Alcohol thirsty.
I'm at your mercy.
My morals and integrity when intact
keep setting me back.
Good finish last.

—

He was good, he wasn't finished, and he passed.
I seen him shot, seen her shot, then I got shot.
Immune to it, those are my immunization shots.
A shot at the bar, shot up the bar, seen dope
shot up in her arm.
Immune to it, those are my immunization shots.
A fiend for this pain, I need morphine for this pain.
Sweat, blood, sex, love.
Everybody's going to die...
Next up?
Hard day and a bad night, deep in this fright.
Realeyes'd I was never even sleep
the nightmare was my life.

GREEN ST.

Spent a night in bookings.
Seen a baby in my dream.
A young kid, he was so young.

> *"Do you know how much time you
> get for a gun?" He asked.*

Three and a half." I told him.

The truth shocked him but he
immediately shook it off smoothly.
He asked me about all that was to come.

*"You look real young, how old are you anyhow?"
I quizzed.*

> *"Eighteen."*

*"Time to grow up now, they're not
playing with them guns." I said dryly.*

> *"Yeah, but I have to keep a gun.
> My brother just died,
> my other brother killed someone.
> I'm probably better off in prison."*

I didn't have a better alternative for him
so I just laid down and
went to sleep with the bed bugs.

N. PARK TO LONG STREET (SHORTCUTS)

We used to put holes
in the gates to take
shortcuts from one block
to the next

Father said, "Shortcuts
always get you where
you don't wanna be."
And so on.

By time he told me that,
a little too late.
I was thirty-three,
a life's span.

Do you know what you
can do in them years?
That's when Jesus met
Calvary.

It took me decades
to Park myself,
to listen anyways.
I'll stay North!

Them Streets entrapped and
sentenced me. From now
on, I'll only take
the Long way!

INSIDE-OUT

Poverty, struggle, pain.
Since life started, that's how it came.
Money, love and fame is what we tried to gain.
Ended up in here, guess we had bad aim.
What would you do if you had bad aim?
This is the shooting range.
You are the target,
target practice.
Practice, practice, practice.
Until you're a sharpshooter,
shooting for the stars.
Shoot! Where do I start?
Right here, right now!
Can you please share how?
Well, you must find that within.
That there is how you win!

INSIDE-OUT 2 (OUTSIDER)

I've been stuck inside but somehow I grew to be an
outsider.
Not ready for the outside world,
feeling confused and lost inside of me.
Trying to figure out where I fit in,
I thought being a loser is how I would win.
Sorry if I confuse you,
so sorry if I abused you
and I am sorry…
If I lose you.
The pain inside is like heavy rain outside,
scared looking for somewhere to duck and hideout.
This is my cry out
before it turns me inside-out.
Now, would you let an outsider in?
I know I have to do better for you, my kin.
A love that's never supposed to end
and that will never die.
After I try to find my way home
after being lost outside.

OUTNUMBERED

"Boom Boom Boom!"

The feds woke him up
to what seemed like his doom,
unfamiliar faces
with guns walking through the living room,
who would have guessed,
that last night literally when he
went to rest,
would be his last taste of freedom
for the next…
some odd years,
this brought on some odd fears,
the ones that made a grown man
taste salty tears,
a man that lacked cry
would be a fat lie,
but no sense of crying about it now,
as the cold air dried them eyes,
I'm a show you how what could've
been one's demise,
turned into a fucking prize,
like pushing yourself with your last breath
to the finish line,
now in first place,
sometimes the best comes up out of
the worsc place,
like the lotus in the mud,
said he was the lowest of a thug,
that dug deep,
the physical and outward presence
of an illusional state
isn't my reality,
so, he studied love

and found his crown in the mud,
power and truth from within
sent him above,
at first it seemed tragic,
but turned into something
good,
that is what we'll call
magic.

SERVING MY PEOPLE

I rode a crowded bus today,
a woman, my elder, got on
reminded me of Rosa Parks, so I gave her my seat.
I was on my way to a school built by Washington—
that's Booker T.
If he could get all that funding right up from slavery,
then maybe
there are no limitations from what I am destined to
be.
Hey beautiful sister, I'm going back to prison.
Need you to be strong like Assata, an educated
woman
like Angela Davis.
If you hold me down like Winnie did Mandela,
I know we'll make it.
And I promise I'll read and study, come home like
Malcolm
with a new light.
Tupac said keep your head up and Bob Marley said
everything's gon be alright.
The greatest said he's not going over there to fight
your war,
"They never called me a nigga" and though I respect
the troops,
I agree with the Greatest,
plus, in my neighborhood, I have to fight my own
war.
That's my duty, teach and feed the youth like the
Panthers did.
Bobby and Huey.
Once I do that, the system will target me,
now jail I go back,
but one day they'll free me like Geronimo Pratt.

Now I left little bro out there— alone, misguided,
love-lacking.
Now he's running up in the courtroom trying to free
me like I'm George Jackson.
Or will I die in jail like Steve Biko?
As long as I die like Martin Luther King Jr.,
serving my people.

GHETTO DEFENDANT

```
United States of America

V.

Mario Finesse Wright


Plea: Insanity

To whom it may concern, (Humanity)

First and foremost, you must know I
was imprisoned way before this
sentence.
Before I was born actually,
because this system was invented to
feed off the indigence.
Even if I was to beat the odds,
it would be odd, because we will
never
be even.
Let alone, I was born to addiction
with cocaine in my system.
Left alone, my mother did stints in
prison
and she was White, there goes my
privilege.
My father also took trips to prison,
I mean traps to prison. He was
Black, that's the trap!
And the trip, well this is our
family vacation.
```

Agony for my younger brothers who
were dependent on me.
I only led them to be co-defendants
to me. Against a prosecution that
celebrates taking down the whole
family.
I don't mean to complain but this is
a… defendant's complaint,
a hopeless appeal from a broken
deal.

The injustices I see!
Why do these phones and commissary
cost so much? As if the tax dollars
you collect to house me isn't
enough?
Are non-violent drug offenses worth
a Covid death sentence?
I could be of better use in these
trying times, especially if you
teach me something!
I see you have the ability to lie.
Correction, Education,
Rehabilitation on a plantation would
be a Lie-ability.
Because why would you want to refine
me to a law-abiding life when you
feed off this here multibillion-
dollar industry.
Could you please tell me, would
farmer free cattle that produces
milk that liquidates his farm?
No!!
All the money in the world and you
continue to want it off my blood,
sweat, and tears.

Even after you've earned, you still
have to keep me for every single
last day of the year. Is it for
monetary gains or for fear?
And I'm not asking for my life to be
spared. That's ok! I don't want your
mercy.
Can't expect leniency from larceny.
It didn't start with me, it won't
end with me, so don't pardon me.
This motion of truth is so you could
come get a taste and a preview, that
one day we will see a switch in
place, and you will…
Free my people!

POOR AUTHORITY

Hey Mr. Officer!

So, what's the difference, you have your drink at the bar,
after work, off the clock. I have mine, open-bottle-container
standing on my block. I only stand out here because I don't
have nowhere else to go. Or sit in the house, no A.C., empty
fridge, with the TV broke? If you really care, set up some
programs for the youth, that'll help the community. Instead,
throw me in jail, teach me a lesson, is what you think it'll do
to me. Little did we know that first time let me know I could handle
anything; it ruined me. Before I started committing crime, I ran
anyway, from my fear of you. Police supposed to protect, lies to me,
because in my neighborhood, I never seen the good you do.
Beclouded Black Cop!
Don't you know this system was created to control us.
I know you think it's different from where we came
from. Well, it did change, from slavery-to
segregation-to mass incarceration. See, it's all the
same, remember in slavery, they had the house nigga
with a little better benefit? Confused, they said
sometimes they forgot which side they were on.

Hey Mr. Judge!

I know I've made wrong decisions, time to pay for
them now. Be careful you don't make the wrong
decisions when you
give me my time. That's a tough job you take,
carelessly deciding
one's fate. Yes, I affected people's lives and I will do
my time.
Understand that any excessive time by you effects my
children more,
now your affecting lives. I accept my responsibility
but the picture the prosecutor is painting isn't always
correct. And I might be paying for my misdoings
now, you might be paying for yours next.

Hey Mr. C.O.!

See how I talk to you with respect, but you
automatically assume because of my situation that I'm
less. Now, if I judge you as a whole, honestly... I
don't like you either. But until you show me
personally your ways, I'm a treat you like people. And
if you wanted to work with animals, you should've
been a zookeeper. I chose my lifestyle, so to blame
you would be ignorant of me. Just like you chose this
job, but why you on the other side of this door more
miserable
than me.

23

See, I was once One that people called on when they
needed help,
officer.
I also was One that made decisions on what to do
when people done wrong like you, judge.
And I once held a lot of keys that opened a lot of
doors, C.O.

But a good person when privileged with some
authority
doesn't let it go to their head and abuses its power.
    Don't shine on the little people, that's Poor
Authority.

JUST BECAUSE THESE VOICES ARE IN MY
HEAD

Just because I come from the slums,
doesn't mean I'll settle for your crumbs.
Never been the settling type.
Just because it used to be drug peddling nights,
doesn't mean better isn't in my eyesight.

I only wanted to be a commodity for this economy.
Scratch that— I mean, for the shares of my
community.
"You can't, you won't!" was said, but I know you lied
to me,
realized that, after years of much scrutiny.

You don't have me fooled.
Just because we dropped out of school,
doesn't mean we lack the talent and the tools,
and out the mud came, the finest of the jewels.

He has a gift! Give him a glove-
because they were pitching, caught felony
convictions
now conflicted
with restrictions
from a system
full of contradiction.

Nah fuck that!
I said.
He was gifted!
Give him some love.

Excuse my language
because it was dangerous

where we was hanging,
though I tamed it,
sometimes the anguish
escapes- in these verbal exchanges.

Or in this written deranged script.
Just because he grew heartless
doesn't mean it was painless.
The pain makes or breaks the heart.

Would he steal, if life was stainless?
He only stole the basics like stolen bases.
These aren't excuses— I'm far from brainless.
Now wouldn't that be heinous.

These are the voices in my head, alright?
They can't take a gift away from you
when it's your passion-
to die for...
And you just might.

A lot of times,
our voices are never heard.
I know they'll put a cap on it
but we can fight!

Is that why we don't have any
young leaders?
Assassinations or suspicious deaths like the-
Bruce Lee-aders.

Is that why we tend to settle more now?
Okay,
okay.

I guess I'll settle it down.

27

PASS THIS KITE TO MY CO-D

Missive No. 1
What's up brodie?
I'm holding up over here like a real one supposed to,
you know me...
You my day-1, we won't let this change none,
remember how we're cut different,
no matter what they say sun.
What I see these dudes on in here,
makes me proud to call you my friend
and just know, good men
will make out in the end.
Sick as it is, the life we chose
comes with these bids.
Are you good on commissary over there?
I know you miss them kids.
Send my love. Kisses and hugs
from they're uncle.
And be militant and safe in case
one of these dudes touch you.
They put a separatee on us so we
don't stick together, strategically.
But even separately,
they not defeating we..
Hold on to the happier times,
the things we been through,
your moms like my moms,
she loves me too.
They just brought the trays around, I been
working out, gotta get to this grub, you know?
Then finish reading this discovery...
                    With Love,
                    You already know!

Missive No. 2
It was good to see you real quick in passing.
It's Ramadan, why you not fasting?
And why haven't you written back?
Someone moved over here from your unit,
said your smoking K2 now,
I heard that's like crack...
Don't let yourself fall victim to that.
We kings bro, I'm hoping you'll bounce back.
Like always, I want the best for you.
But I'm not gonna lie, I'm not feeling the vibes,
and the times, that's testing you.
Since kids, it was "never let them see you sweat"
and definitely no folding up.
You asked, how I'm holding up?
I'm studying bro, making sure each day I
learn something through it all.
I mean you're supposed to get up, brush off,
and learn from the misstep, after you fall.
Heard you got into a little brawl...
Remember, if your minds not sharp,
you can't win at all.
Make sure you're working out and
staying mentally strong.
A cat over here I thought was official,
whole time, he was singing a song.
I just don't understand when one turns on
his own, knowing he wrong...
                    Until next time my brother,
                              I'm gone!

A Response
Sorry bro, I haven't been writing.
Was really stuck on what I was deciding.
The lawyer said, we gotta look out for ourselves.
I didn't know being locked up, felt like hell.

———

I miss my girl, alone in this cell.
You could get less time too,
if you'd tell...
I aint getting no mail.
No one answering the phone.
I hope you understand bro,
I gotta go home...
                    Later bro.

Missive No. 3 (Final Words)
You caught me off guard with that,
don't know what to say, how to react.
All I know is, it pierced my heart
when you stabbed me in my back.

BARS AND CONCRETE

(Essex Co. NJ)
The first three years, exciting
under the influence
how you fought that pain
drunks fighting
many losses
but how we found it fun
is hard to explain

or understand, on one hand
with poverty, crime and
unemployment
makes sense, how one can
soak in that enjoyment

it was joint with a liquor store
also connected to a bodega
standing at the counter
like staring into a diverse audience
all the different brands and flavors

good vibes, inside
everyone welcome, everything's alright
old school dropping drunk jewels
while staggering on the stool
that old-day smell
freed a dopamine
a quick escape from hell

take it back to your block
standing on your corner
"What did you bring?"
Could tell what it was in the
black plastic bag from the

way it 'clink-clinked'

the sidewalks you stood on
saw everything under the sun
if you felt as if you didn't have a life
or weathered a harder one
somehow you thought the
sidewalks rebirthed you
or just made it better
but only gave you
a harder one

(Federal Prison)
These first three years
you don't even want to wake up
like you could sleep it all away
how you fought that pain
but if metal drains
a battery's life, wouldn't me laying
on this metal bed, do the same?

these bars enslave,
and this concrete plays
with your mind
why do the walls sweat?
and they stand upright while
you're on your back,
thinking back...
it switched positions from when you
use to stand outside in the trap

now your trapped
surrounding confining abandoned souls
with no escape
sure wish you could get that drink now
after this harsh taste of reality

use to regret them, now you wouldn't
mind a hangover

but these
bars and concrete
make the natural
high of life…
now sober.

RUFF RYD'N

I didn't have to walk the yard with a great,
to realize I was great.
Just helped me understand
though it's dark and hell is hot,
I could still shine bright
and be the man.
Never been the type to be up under the next person,
no matter whatever.
So, we probably would of never spoke,
if we didn't ride in together.

This isn't admiration,
just a little inspiration.
See, I been slipping since a child,
I fell and you told me to get back up.
Through trials and tribulations,
life's up and downs,
I learned it's gon' pick back up.
I gotta salute you
for the days your music helped me get through
and hoping one day, for my people,
I could do the same too.

LEFT ON THE CLOTHES-LINE

Lost in prison
not where I want to be
lost my vision
but my eyes can still see,

but my I's are closed
because nobody wants me
and nobody knows
except the ruins of We,

phone only did ring
what had seemed like forever
never did they bring,
mailman done lost the letter

is it true that love and friendship
really do go rotten.
or is it not by intention
just simply forgotten?

CONFUSION

My trust issues
fed my lust issues
I'm a live how I want to,
I'm like fuck issues
too weak to discuss issues
not the type to cuss with you

and fuss with you
I wanted you
but felt like I was stuck with you
I was thinking backwardly
that was the battered me,
the sadder, the greedy, the fatter me

a love tragedy

ALLY

A poem for a friend while I sit in the hole.
First and foremost, I admire your blossoming soul.
A genuine gracious connection is my goal.
In a Nick of time, we already rhyme, our words
have their own rhythm.
I really like them; I know you dig them.
Back to the matter at hand which is you!
Your distinct style is dope,
you don't even try, it's true.
The ground should be happy when your stepping
on it, flaunt it...
I'm sure it's a sight to see, a vibration to feel.
Keep them vibes, stay joyful and great things
you're sure to do.
Hopefully, I can ride along and see it through.

BLACK BIRD

I seen birds fly by the hundreds.
Dirty pigeons in the streets where I come from,
to a beautiful lone pigeon on a mountain
in West Virginia.
Do birds still fly south for the winter or did
they learn to survive in the cold?
Do birds in the ghetto know they're in the ghetto?
And are they free?
Free as a bird they say.
But not a jailbird.
A beautiful bird isn't as beautiful in a cage.
Like a crow in rage,
plucking at his feast.
Be brave,
because if you're chicken,
life looks scarce the way these beasts eat.
There's no bird-feeding or peaceful chirping.
Don't sing bird, because them birds are hurting.
That's how I seen birds die by the hundreds.

GOOD MORNING (FROM A PRISON WINDOW)

I awoke today! Always a good start.
I lay in my bed looking out the window at a serene
sky.
It's still dark and the moon is full.
The moon disappears completely in the clouds
And once the clouds clear, the moon glows.
The sky is a dark blue.
I would need a big crayon box with labels to know
the precise color. The moon is a yellowish white like
a light.
The clouds start to smother the moon again.
I say smother because when the clouds
go into the light, they're a dark gray.
It looks like the smoke
that comes from the top of a factory building
in a city when you pass by it on a highway.
How could something polluted
look exactly like something so beautiful?
The moon survives the smothering as the clouds pass
by again.
I thought I seen a big star close to the moon,
and stars seem to be so rare nowadays.
But as I moved in my bed,
I noticed it was just a speck in the window.
Amazed me how the speck shined just like a star,
again, how could something so dirty look so perrty?
Two ft. below the moon, the clouds, and the speck,
stood the top of the trees,
I meditated on how these things could be so far
from one another,
but from my outlook, so close in the same picture.
The wind started to sing through the window cracks
as the sun danced his way in.
I seen the sun and moon together in the sky

---

like lovers passing by.
Even though the bars in the window tried to ruin the
marvelous view.
Even though I wouldn't leave the cell to get a good
whiff of it,
I knew today would be a good day
as I realized how precious life truly is.

LOVELY NATURE

Does the night envy the day?
Do the grass blades get stuck on individuality
and fight each other
or do they drink the rain together,
relaxing in the sun?
Does one tree get jealous because the other
is taller or smaller?
Are they loyal to the soil?
When times get hard, do leaves have a
choice to stay or leave?
Do the waves steal?
I wouldn't mind them taking me away.
Would I be missed?
Does the air ever grieve because it is
a forevery kiss?
And revenge!
Is it man-made or animal instinct?
Are animals forgiving?
Is the plant kingdom kinder
than mankind?
Does it cherish time?
Do the stars shoot at each other to shine the brightest?
Shooting stars!
Was the apple evil?
If alchemy can work in unity,
why can't we?
Misery is-
you and me?
Are we supreme or
are We the insanity?
Either way
I still love our nature.

RAINY DAY

The raindrops came and I ducked for cover
The raindrops came but I broke the umbrella
The raindrops came and made the day so gloomy
The raindrops came and coldly it moved me
The raindrops came so I sped up my pace,
running away as the raindrops
were coming down her face.

HOW DANDY

1

Early in the morning,
the dandelion opened
his eye.
By late afternoon,
they're all gone-
like a 9 to 5.

2

The end of a school day,
are there too many hours
in a day?

3

Unless there's much rest
needed to serve their
purpose in life.
It worsens because
they'll never know
how fun it is at night.

LONGING ON A LONG DAY

If I could be
in this moment
of your acquaintance.

What would it be,
no composure
or physical patience?

Feels like my insides
wanna hug you,
before I explode!

Very gratified-
to have loved you,
deep within my soul.

BARBED-WIRED FENCES

Forty-four geese
I calculate.
It's stand-up count
or advocate.

Why are you here?
Inside these gates,
do you not know freedom?
Not in your mind-state?

If never confined,
free— you wouldn't know.
Don't shake your tail feather
at me, just go!

Cut the grass to dine,
brawn necks turning,
chase your own away-
eating earnest.

Do you notice
the sad faces here?
As long as it's feed,
you don't care.

We both have something
in common, wallow.
In the belly of the beast,
greed is sure to follow.

QUARANTINE WISH

Hey Nature,

Is Covid lying?
Excuse my ignorance,
I know we're dying.
But look at you, Dandelion.
Standing so tall in the Fall.
If mankind wipes out,
I bet you'll withstand it all.
Unlike Us...
You must only put good-
out into the world,
with your good nature
and your goodwill too.
Unlike Us...
And when you are taken
away from your world,
not because I hate you-
but I have killed you.
I mow the lawn
until you're all gone.
Or a selfish pluck
to make a wish,
then discard your corpse
to the sticks.
You've drowned as
floods destroyed towns.
Is that man-made or a
natural disaster?
As I pass ya,
admiring how you persevere.
How you dance in the wind
with no fear.
A promise to you-

my little friend,
no matter how sick I become-
I'll never pick at you
again…

47

FREEDOM I MISS

The pleasure I miss
like wind blowing me a kiss
a chill from the Winter brisk
or a light gentle mist,

Warmth turning to the Summer heat
leaves keeping in the street
raindrops making a beat
and slush playing at my feet,

The sun at his favorite hour
still dries off after a quick shower
brightens the Earth with his power
and raised up a beautiful flower,

Darkness stalking the night
then everything turning white
off the skinny tree branches
even when the storm dances.

SAPPHO MADE A PASS AT ME

Quill in hand, passion leaked
to acquire is grand
word travels through love, passage leads
way above
transcribed scripts, passes to thy king
pages of gifts

like a Greek poet

silent art passionately
opened a heart
mind fought passed the weeks
pondered in ocean thought
to touch thee, gently, passively,
heavenly

like a Greek goddess

VISIT

I see your face gleaming
is it because I'm your man
and we're a team

Let's see if we're dreaming
give me your hand
yeah, it's what it seems

An extraordinary love story
that doesn't end
how many past lives saw
this glory
and when did it begin

For you
make me shine too
my lady lover friend.

HAVE YOU EVER

Seen a man cry?
I did.
I've seen stubborn eyelids-
give in and turn violent.
Marching down his face.
Seemed as if he was displaced.
Did something die inside?
Was it the image one
tried to uphold?
To be tough and bold?
Life only seemed to be cold,
since genesis.
His mask off, defenselessness
from his nemesis.
Was it grief, underneath-
that skin?
Precious green world
supposed to be a
releaf—
what happened?

Release them!

What's been bottled up since birth,
must hurt— now it's open.
Like a letter in a bottle traveling
the earth— floating,
taking too many twists and turns
lost in the ocean.

Release them!

To appreciate just the travels
would alleviate or eliminate

unraveling half the battle.

Bad ruins or good measures,
that's tears for the years,
evil-doings or good gestures,
that's fear of the tears,
humble or aggressor,
that's tears everywhere,
love is our pleasure,
that's cheers through the tears!

Be careful straddling the fence,
you might tear a testicle,
poor ol'dude.
Up to you what side you choose,
just use,
your intestinal fortitude.

Holding that lie,
you were deprived,
it's okay to cry…
Now you're alive!

PUSH

Some days when I awake,
I feel like shutting down
but I get up anyhow
and push forward
to my highest
capability

UPSTAIRS IN THE ADDICT

Your soon to be released from the zoo
but the monkey is on your back.
Fight, I said fight!
Get him off you.
Denial is your dull sword and pity is
your worn-down shield that won't
protect you anymore.
All them years to reflect on yourself
and the monkey has taken away any
progress you've thought you've made.
Be strong and fight, I said fight!
He's eating you alive.
The real world is not going to cater
to the weak.
Okay, you got him now.
Wait!
Why are you holding him down?
He'll never tap out; you have to finish him!
Damn, he has you again, in a headlock,
You're losing consciousness.
Society is whooping you now, brain-dead,
you're as good as gone.
I foolishly hope you recover
but you won't, because you are the monkey
on your back.

STILL ANGRY 55 YEARS LATER (FOR GEORGE FLOYD)

Like Watts in 65, how many more died before the
world cried?
Hundreds, thousands, hundreds of thousands?
Police Brutality... Finally reveals racism by a mishap.
A cop kneels, a cop shoots and the streets loot, call in
the troops!
Thought we would just sit and watch on social media
while we're
stuck in the house being wiped out by someone's
plandemic.
Your miscalculation broadened it, your secret is
internationally
known, our whole life been a pandemic.
I'd rather die with reverence, so I put my mask on and
head out in
the storm because my community been unemployed.
The deadly virus daunts any hope I had of better days
and if it
doesn't kill me, a pig will.
Protesting next to a white woman, my ally, we threw
a rock for
Emmett Till.
But does she really know everything that's going on,
like how
prison = slavery or how I was targeted as a baby?
A cop's personal inner hate is only the social order's
domino effect.
Police Brutality...is America's racism in its bottom-
shelf form.
The pinnacle is unknown. Chemical warfare, mass
incarceration,
political, economic, social racism.

I was fooled to fight in Vietnam against those fighting for freedom
when I wasn't even free.
I was fooled to sell drugs, gangbang and destroy people that were
just like me.
I was fooled and schooled by a disparaged biased education.
Targeting our parents to become addicts imprisoning the next
generation.
Yeah, yeah, the same blame game.
No! If you dig deep, you'll see the facts and the history of our system.
Just like if you dig deep, you'll see the closeness between the victor
and the victim.
After the riots in the 60's and the 70's found ways to calm us down
or dumb us down.
Aggressive, fiery, strong, masculine BLACKMAN!
Now a political prisoner, or a crackhead, or just subdued, sick
feeding off your fast food that's also killing me…
Until I'm fed up!
Half a century later, we fight again, now what will you do?
Change?
How about a new declaration?
Or more lies, more trickery?
I figured.
What's new?
Guess you have to give the devil his due.
We will never give up,
how about you?

RACISM

We both had a love for art as we vibed in my cell,
I'm talking about the Mexican tattooing my body,
more than cordial as I took a liking to him,
as we laughed together today— erasing sorrow,
but tomorrow,
brings adverse times as we stand in the middle of a
riot,
I stand with my comrades and you with yours
Mexicans with Mexicans
Blacks with Blacks
Whites with Whites
quick cruel turn of events,
uncertain hatred that's always awaiting,
craving for confrontation.

In the depth of my heart
I know you're just like me
poverty raised
just like me
family man
just like me
I see you struggling
just like me
in the same situation
just like me
I can go on and on because in many ways
you're just like me.

No need to look at you as an enemy
we got bigger problems in the world
and the color of one's skin nor a
language barrier or a Trump wall,
should stop one good man from
connecting with another

but that's just the way it is.

Sounds like just a prison setting
but it goes on in every suburban
or inner-city neighborhood
across the globe
Why do ill thoughts cross minds when
you see people that differ?

No solution or happy ending to this one
because it's just the way it is,
so, I'll just end this by stopping…

IS VIOLENCE NECESSARY?

I'd say so
United States said so
the conqueror said so
the Europeans said so
Black on Black said so
the judges' sentence said so
the death penalty said so
it's all dreadful

If they hit you, hit them back
mama said so
pain said so
Cane said so
to Abel
turn the other cheek
I'm not able
because The Panthers said so
and Malcolm said so
only because the kkk said so
and police brutality says so
a lot of uniforms said so
even the storms said so
and the wars said so
the rich and the poor said so
when will we let go?

Do I even have a say so?
Because history said so
and science said so
Covid said so
even the bible said so
King David said so
animal kingdoms say so
the aggressor said so

the oppressor said so
and then the revolutionary
said so
devils said so
hate said so
seems like even love
sometimes says so.

All I wanna know,
does God have a say so?

DIAMONDS

Chest ever get warm
heart start beating fast
hope it wasn't a heart attack
I'm too young for that
chest pains
heart ache
last time it pounded like that
I was stuck between a rock
and a hard place
like a stolen car chase
my bad, I'm from Jersey
that's the hard place
and the rock was what my parents
was smoking when I was born
that got my chest hurting
in the first place
asthmatic
ass-backward
running from a slave dungeon
in Ghana
400 years ago
to end up in a jail cell in
AmerikkkGo-to hell
scared to seek medical attention
from the ones holding me
against my will
for the pain in my chest
I guess I'll just sleep on it
If I die, I think it'll be a
cardiac arrest…

2020 VISION

The virus assassinates optimism weakening 98% of
everyone,
one way or another.
She would say you have nice nails noticing my
manicure.
Neither the simplest things in life
nor the more significant— don't matter,
nothing does when the world is upside down
change falling from its pocket.
Delirious gave her a ride and drove her off a
cliff…but she'll live. Children miss dinner waiting on
dessert, deserted cities,
We're all facing a deadly drought like stranded in a
desert.

Lonely days
gloomy days
sick days
make me wonder…
I shouldn't have
smoked them cigarettes
and drank and drugged
and wasted time
and went to jail
I should have
ate more healthy
and took my vitamins
and wore a condom
and saved some money
and took care of myself
and spent more time with my family
and cherished it all…

Well now I know and if I don't deteriorate and I
survive the madness,
I'll be that 2%.

63

MY IRRATIONAL THOUGHTS

Nov 2020

"Good morning, Mrs. C.O"
"Good morning Mr. Wright"
"See we got a new President."
"Yeah, as long as he don't mess with my money, I
don't have a problem with it"

"So that's all it's about?" I wondered.

Ignorance is bliss
you goofy bi***
I don't mean to disrespect
but when she said this
I felt a wayward diss
awoke on the bright side
but allowed it to shift.
What did I miss?
What about Covid-19?
What about the sick?
My body tensed
let me tap into my thoughts
before I inappropriately vent
see if I could calm my emotions
before I regret what happens next.
"Look at the job she has
what do you expect?"
That's what was said in my head
my body relaxed
as I felt perplexed
One's selfishness shouldn't be so surprising
my helplessness is becoming depriving
but after realizing
that it won't be my demise

I hurried off smiling.

"Good day Mrs.C.O"

65

LIKE GEESE IN THE WINTER

So cold and lonely
with warm wishes
as I clutch my
blanket with you
lying beside me
only in my
head.

Haven't had sexual
relations in years
may have forgotten
how unless
it's like driving
a car
once you get in
and the feel of it
accelerating lightly
as you take control
picking up speed
before you know it
you are at your
destination happily
I always was a good driver.

Love sounds I don't remember
no longer does that music play
in my head
can't wait to dance
to the sweet melodies
if I still have rhythm
I always had my own style anyway.

It's been years
I said
I have to close my eyes to see it
but it's still too dark
breathing in and out of my nose
trying to get a whiff of you
but distance and time
have gotten too far ahead of me
my taste buds lost until they're found
by a serving of your beauty
rejuvenating all five of my senses.

Pornographic pictures are a quick fix
that makes me sick to my stomach
because it's not the special someone
who prizes me in my daydreams
as I multiply my past
memories
with my future plans
along with my creative lust
as I patiently wait
but in the meantime
it is so cold and lonely.

Dear AmeriKKKa,

Kindly Kiss me, who you Kidding, just to Kick me down. That's how my Kinfolk was Kidnapped. Kill the dignity of my Kinsmen so my Kinswomen can work in your Kitchen, taking my Kids for your Keepsake tying a Knot in them since Kindergarten.

Knapsacks of Kilos dropped to my Kindred as neighborhoods Kindled away. Trying to play Ketchup chasing your Knick Knacks with a Knife in our backs and a Knee on our necks to Kill us or put us in Khaki suits Keeping us down was the Key.

King me! Watch me raise up Keen Knights that will never Kneel. Full of Knowledge ready to Knuckle up or Karate fight until your power gets Knocked out. You could keep your Kudos but we'll take the Karats and back to the Kingdom my Kin go.

MAYA

Wish I was there to protect you
Even though you're more so my ancestor
Did trauma make you great?
I couldn't help you regardless
N'even there for my own daughters
And right now, they're eight...

MISS YOU

My Lady,

I miss you, a feeling almost
as if it's unfair.

But as we know
an uncut jewel is most rare.

And to miss it is to only care.

In addition, with some lonely fear.

Joyful as it is, a mutual share.

Thoughts of you harass me
everywhere.

As I proudly
patiently wait…
To one day,
smell your hair.

JUST PLAYING W/ WORDS

Curiosity picks at intelligence
as it seduces.
An intelligent mind is also
a filthy one,
what a nuisance…
Guess there's
a positive
and negative
in all
Some attract to intelligence
with no care for filth
while
intelligence intimidates
some who prefer filth
To have what you want
you have to know a balance
in it all…
Well,
I'll have
a double shot
mixed!
And
she'll have the same.

STREET EDUCATED

Growing up, he took to it like the school system.
Until he was cuffed off to college. That's where he
advanced his learning or completely dropped out.
Tutors— nobody bothered.
Adolescence, it was the basics…Watching his family
get high in the basement, empty dope bags on the
pavement. Observing, on his time, he was waiting.
This learning was concerning, taking mental notes
without even noticing. They said he chose it, or did
life do the choosing? At ten, in school with grown
men. Looking up to them until they would let him in.
Blocks were the hallways.
Social class— absent because in the ghetto,
everybody fits in. On the same playing field unless
you was nice on the football field.
Math was the first subject given, a necessity with no
financial aid. For the hungry, lunch money to get fed.
Strategy was picked up avoiding the police raid. He
fled for physical ed.
Awareness and curiosity on why he was so numb in
the slum gave him history lessons on civil rights, to
slavery, to world order, to how his mind was a
weapon.
Whether passed or failed, he moved on because the
fast life doesn't stand still. Still held back.
Whether excel or expelled, he took it as an experience
with hope not to get X'd out, like his friends that were
exiled.
No homecomings and socials made him antisocial
until he found a bar. Pints, liters, gallons he raised the
bar.
A road test in a stolen car didn't take him far.

Enough!

Too much negative static, time to advance the
mathematics. Families divided simplifies prison, no
more division in his vision. He chose to stand up to
the school bully in his mind. His smarts were too
powerful, understanding the rational in due time.
No class clown.
Science was his body and spirit, things they didn't
teach in school, he started to cherish.
Fuck a cap and gown, a crown, he would wear it!

To graduate is to elevate from the madness. Street
education establishes
the strongest individuals.
Sadness
for so many it never happens.
As he found the reciprocal, the pain and the gain.
Studying more became critical
As he evaluated the exam.
Impoverished boy to a wealthy man.
Congratulations to the street educated!

FREE-DEM

Let me out of this cell
and I'll jump from the slave ship,
the cold-water cooling
me off from this burning hell,

so I could find heaven in her
again, my favorite sin.
Are we close,
hardly, shackles scarring me

my own hand
my own land
my own plan
my own Man

free the mind
free the child
free the people
free-dem!

HELP IS ON THE WAY

An institution scene
a sobering bad dream.
Caffeine, my only friend-
my only fiend.

Adding to the dehydration.
Covid nineteen,
eliminates visitation—
that's love elimination.

The days of no response,
you oxymorons!
Time for a formation,
reform the reformatory—

So young boys and girls
won't have to continue this story...

MANIFESTING

I've been working towards this my whole life.
Live in the moment, I'd rather not.
Because the moment shifts every time your wrist
watch, tick-tocks, and blood constantly flows through
the same vein.
So shouldn't I modify until I die?
And maybe following
when we return to the essence.
It's all a transition like a seed that is planted,
grows, dies and used for whatever
thereafter.
Life's a never-ending chapter
in one big book.
We always were and we'll always be.
To sit dormant would go against nature,
Making you guilty God,
this isn't a puzzle, no mystery earth.
Just push and strive
learn to master
eat and feed
your spiritual
your mental
to grow and develop
as you accelerate to
elevate.

SENECA VILLAGE

Would you like to help me change the world?
Come on... We must come together.
That way we can make it through whatever.
Let's start with all the little girls,
we will love and protect them.
Show them that the boys 2 men will respect them.
Yeah, the troubled little boys,
Ritalin isn't going to check them,
fathers got to step in,
teach them, love them, correct them.
Black or white,
Why is the opposite race scared of ya?
Black or white,
so many lonely kids in America.
I know because I was one.
You know what I mean..
Black and white,
stuck in between,
a lost teen.
Who wants me?
Plus, the things I've seen,
almost turnt me into a fiend,
but prison wants me.
Exposure to a wounded culture,
turnt me into a vulture.
That's what we have to take care of,
so many broken homes in America,
time to tear them down,
and rebuild them to fly.
Don't turn a blind eye,
just because yours is all fine and dandy.
Lend a helping hand, to the insanity.
Come on... Will you hold hands with me?
Sing, cheer and dance with me?

I do my part, you do your part,
that's where we start.
Love is the anthem.
A unity mantra.
together, together, together,
this will advance us.

GRANDMA BOUGHT A HOME

I want to buy a home
and pay it off first
I want to buy a home
So I could never pay rent again, fattening the
next man's purse
I want to buy a home
So I could be on my way to financial freedom
I want to buy a home
So poverty I could beat him
I want to buy a home
So I could build some equity
I want to buy a home
with good schools and good neighbors
next to me
I want to buy a home
So I could fix it to my liking and do what I
please with it
I want to buy a home
comfortably, without someone seizing it
I want to buy a home
and build a pool with a garden, now that a
be peaceful
I want to buy a home
and throw a big cookout, invite 360 people
I want to buy a home
So my kids can have a nice backyard to play in
I want to buy a home
So I could put my toys in the garage, that a be
my playpen
I want to buy a home
So I could make extra money, renting
out parking spaces or the basement
I want to buy a home
So when the city comes, I could have a say-so

———

like "re-do the pavement!"
I want to buy a home
So I could add it to my worth
I want to buy a home
So I could own a peace of this earth
I want to buy a home
just to sit on the porch like my grandma use to
I want to buy a home
and you should too…

MY APOLOGY TO A WOMAN

 I was asleep...

I knew your beauty, so absolute on the inside, all I did
was take advantage.
This masculine society surrounding us gave me the
misconception on what manhood was.
Lost, I treated you as less taking you for granted.
Your soul spoke innocence, honesty, and passion.
You said, "Come with me." I ignored you and turned
away.
"Wait, I can love you!" you cried out.
Viciously, I turned back. "Who are you and what
language is this you speak?"
"You're unworthy, what do you know?" I retorted.
 Not knowing how important you are to this earth, I
caused you tears as you tried to nurture me.
I confused you, abused you and misused you.
Knowingly I deserved to lose you.
Still lacked knowledge, as you were an asset, I chose
not to invest in truth.
My life of many liabilities made my choices poor.

Then I awoke...

After they dug a hole in a mountain and I stumbled
and fell in, you searched for me,
day-in, day-out, trying to rescue me.
I was stuck where the lonely resides, perishing from
the hunger of life.
You jumped down with me, ensuring me it was
alright,
keeping me alive.
Enemies informed me my being was insignificant and
broken. I was convinced.

Until you fixed my crown, revealing me to the truth.
Almost in defeat, their mental trickery, their laws, the
odds were all beating me down.
You pulled them off me, gifting me with a
superpower and the strength to fight. "Get up king!"
you commanded.
Your voice fed energy to my heart. As I recollected
who I was and my purpose, I stood tall and awakened.
Conscious and courageous supplied only by love. I
heard you, understanding everything from the
beginning.
Embarrassed by my blunder. Your purpose was to
revive me.
I was ignorant no more.

Compensation...

Now that you cured me, I'm a man together with a
woman and we design life.
With a duty to protect all the little princesses in the
world from fools like the one I once was and their
wickedness.
Even when you feel weak, find your power.
I fathom your pain, I understand you.
And then you fell in distress. I caught you embracing
your hand and helped you up.
"I'll carry you queen." I proudly stated.
The most gorgeous smile broke through the agony on
your face like the sunshine breaking through the
clouds after a tempest.
"You're strong now." You blushed.
"Thank you. You helped me get here. I'm sorry I
didn't have it before to provide for you."
I ended.

SON

 What have I done son?
Brought you into this world
and left you to face it on your own,
Now you don't want to talk,
I feel you looking at me wrong,
I know you don't understand,
you just know something's missing,
I'm dead,
chose another woman,
drugs got a hold of me,
or I'm just off in prison,
generation after generation,
it passes on,
so please understand this game,
my pop failed to teach me things,
I thought I'd do better
but ended up doing the same,
now you act out,
attention and trouble is how you ease the pain,
look, that's how I was…
see it's happening all over again,
just chill, be wiser and please don't let your
mind idle,
one day, you will be a man with a son
and you will change the cycle.

SISTER HAD IT HARD

Like a rose that grew in a neglected garden
disheartened, from the start and—
broken innocence caused the petals to harden
maybe ignorance could have pardoned
but since she was smart and—
observed,
she seen things no one
deserved,
no moping around because hope was found,
even though she lived in a
broken town
veered off the road of excuses
excuses are useless
a bad drive
stinging over and over
like living in
a beehive.

Do you think she had it easier?
She is a girl.
Yeah, I'd say,
if this was Disney's World.
Little princess.
"Can I fix your hair?" mother out of style.
Trouble everywhere,
brothers running wild
an unusual habitat
daddy in his Cadillac
home alone
if he phoned home
it might stop me at the right timing
before this older guy breaks into my hymen.

Look in the mirror-Her

don't be scared of her
pain gives character
Misses America
would you erase it,
if it was abrasive-
or head-on face it?
Would you open-arm
embrace it?
It is what made you, you!
Wouldn't life be tasteless
if you changed faces,
from destiny's cadence
I sure wouldn't replace it,
especially not you!

LITTLE BROTHER

O! How I look up to you.
I'm no Nestor of the clan
because I am no better man.
We are both men of rectitude.
Strong, powerful and
respectable.
They will salute us both.

The world will applaud you
as it sings me a hymn.
Was Agamemnon greater
or less than Menelaus,
because a few years
separated them?

No! They were both kings!

O! How I admire you the same.
As we fight adversity,
enjoying talks with you.
Though afflictions came,
still a pure pleasure
walking along side of it with you.

Souls have families too, traveling
through different times together.

Coming on this journey to learn through life,
purposes differ and some souls
are older and wiser than others.

One thing's for sure
our similarities and how we role
you are

mint to be my little brother.

FOUR YOU

Four precious hands
in a month's span
in a hospital operating
on a heart

once revived,
he opened his eyes
a flare of love
was sparked

now able to smile
so worth its wild
never again
would he depart

DON'T GO

Piece of me will decay
if you go away
our love was
supposed to
stow away

In no way
form or fashion
will I let this happen
please don't go
is what I'm asking

ABOUT LAST NIGHT

My firefly is out of sight
After parting, I felt a
nostalgic aching

love and missing must
be siblings the way
they stick together

an unfair fight, two against
one, except if all goes well
then it's a threesome

painting a picture of her and
playing her voice only in
my head, miserably

my heart froze like Jack
and Rose, that's how love
stories end

I've read about this, so this
is what Rumi meant when
he spoke on grief

WELCOME (FOR ADAM AND GERALDIN)

What an experience…
When new life acquaints
itself with the world
at your doing Mr. Gardener.

Your own personal creation,
like a seed one sowed.
Now you're the decision maker
on how to water it with love and watch him grow!

And your special design
like molding clay,
Mrs. Pottery Maker.
Made in your own beautiful way.

Motherhood. Fatherhood.
Like an important job, with the best position,
bringing meaning and purpose
on this new day, as this new joy is gifted.

LIKE YOU MORE THAN A FRIEND

Sometimes I feel there's some words
I need and want to express,

At that moment, holding it in makes
me feel a bit compressed,

For only with you I feel no need to
rush what's inside of my chest,

Because we both understand the feeling
we share as if we passed the test,

I hear it from you without you speaking
and that there's the best!

TAKE ME TO ANOTHER LOVEL (IN THE CURRENT)

Rare, profound and intense
once I found that wish
it defined love and miss
with a taste so rich

she was someone's daughter
wondering how I caught her
mind flooded with water
as she was all I thought of

though I felt a future sign
and we talked backward time
as she captured my mind
a true feeling of mine

we chose to live in the moment
made life like moaning
test drive and I had to own it
didn't care where we were going

thinking how I met you
the flood, she was my rescue
a flood of sexual
a love of intellectual

if she crashed, I'm safety
as nothing breaks, WE
that's how she takes me
to another lovel baby.

KISSING IN THE FLOWERS

Parked under a tree
a lay
in between
the silky grass

and the winds melody
blew through its
green hairs
with such a care

accompanied by the
dandelions
standing proud

as the sun
looked around,
the fruits of it all
so
Godly
the outlandish innocence
of her nature

from afar I
spotted a
big butt fox

then I placed my
mouth on you
and that's when I knew
that I was eating my
last orange.

EIGHT QUESTIONS

Will the hairs on
your body give us a
standing ovation
as we kiss?

Will the butterflies
swim in your stomach
when we exchange?

Will our electricity
light up the world
as I connect my
power to yours?

Will it be sinful
if the kids hear
this lullaby?

Aren't we already
brutish with you
on all fours?

Aren't we the ocean,
the sun and heaven—
when we blend?

Is this what our
soul came here
to accomplish?

Isn't love
everything?

TWO GOLD MEDALISTS

Hearts
raced

feeling yours
pounding closely
made mine speed
breaths panting
sharing kisses
the best hydrate
a sip from the soul
and let it rain back
down on your pothole
where the
pretty pink flower
stood
you felt the wind
as I passed,

I reached back
handpicking
you with
caresses, and
finger-licking
so you could
cum along
bodies sweating yearning
for the
finish-line
yet this
lovemaking
wins and is
never-ending...
Our trophy!

GO DOWN THERE

If you were the Earth, I would go down there and
swim in your ocean and breathe your air.

If you were a car, I would go down there and
drive you wild.

If I was a car, I would go down there and
let you ride.

If you were a drink, I would go down there and
drink your juices.

If you were food, I would go down there and
eat until I couldn't eat no more.

If you were a dancer, I would go down there and
let you dance on me.

If you were a killer, I would go down there and
let you suffocate me.

If you were a school, I would go down there and
study and learn everything about you.

If you were a queen, I would go down there and
serve your majesty.

Please let me know what you are so I could find
my reason to go down there!

PERFECT

Some say no one is perfect. I say we are all perfectly
made the way we are supposed to be, in our own way.
God created us this way to learn and grow through
our mistakes, flaws and yes— imperfections.
Therefore, we are who and what we are created to be
and that there's perfect!
So, as we embrace our own perfection, we come to
the understanding of the next person's all-around
beauty, inside and out, in their own perfect way.
Seeing this in them is understanding who they are and
accepting them for that.
What about when another's perfection fits you? As
rare and as difficult as it is, it must be special. One of
the most precious things in the world is finding
someone that's perfect for you.
That's what we will call our perfect love thing!

KISSES FROM A KING

Encouragement and enlightenment
is all I want to entrust every day,
please embrace it.
Semblance will never achieve, face it.
He lost his mind! I'll admit—
a few times, I misplaced it.
Internal triumph is being able to look in the
mirror without any disgraces.
External blemishes are fine.
"You're fine!" said Finesse.
It gives you character, if you look at it
with a little understanding.
A little distinction is what makes you. You!
Now you're outstanding!
What is the norm anyway?
I'd rather be an outlier,
because an outsider
Sounds freer to me.
Superpowers come from within—
like, he's genuine!
A man of moral.
An honest woman.
He was only a hoodlum
because of his environment.
She only desires him
because her life was deprived and—
then he started to study, became knowledgeable
and her experiences, made her wisdom flow.
Greatness is in us all, we just have to tap in.
Or wake up on a park bench 50 years later
like, "what happen?"
Surely, he didn't do it on purpose.
Some of us just have different purposes.
You have to find out what's subscribed to you.

And remember to find that out,
just look inside of you.

100

DRUG DEALER VS. POET

I was a better hustler than I am a writer.
I was good at getting straight to the point
when I handled my business living fast.
Not so good at sitting still, literature and going into
detail,
I'll probably finish last.
Drugs medicated the pain, my poems can do the
same,
I'm still your prescriber.
Rather give the people something positive as I switch
the
game, I still serve fire!
But the streets keep calling and writers blocked my
number,
if I answer, they'll say I'm dumb and dumber.
You can't sniff or smoke this, but I can write you
something
erotic and still take you to ecstasy.
Maybe I'll even enlighten you through my word,
sharing something I've learned.
Instead of fighting you on the curb because one of us
got burned.
And they'll still lock me up if I get too influential.
It's okay, I never minded taking risks, that's
evidential,
but we have to add something good to our credentials.
I did, I threw away my scale and picked up my pencil.

DRUG DEALER VS. POET 2

I used to love money
now I love this.
When the words shift
from my wrist
or come out of my lips
like a kiss.
You can't kiss no dirty
money, you'll get
blisters on
your lips.
I just hope everyone
finds something they
love,
that would
be my last wish…

LOST CHILD

I do this for the ghettos
the imprisoned rebels
the lower levels
the ten-year-old
clearing your driveway in the cold
with a broken shovel.

Better treat him right
or he'll be back to steal your bike
wonder if they ever wondered
what his life was like.
Wonder no more
because half of them kids
aren't living no more...

What they could have done
is measureless
because when this is where you're from
you become dexterous.
Oh! Watch the pivot,
how I switch from ignorant
just because you haven't taught me shit
doesn't mean I'm a nitwit!
Yeah, he learned no limits.

Master P the teacher
and I'm the feature
and you're the future
don't let prison defeat ya'
find reading a leisure

Your mind is fruitful
open your eyes
blind and beautiful

now crimes seducing you
and time subduing you
just open your I's…

104

VACCINATE ME

IF this vaccine kills me,
I'll be back to get you back.
A bad feeling fills me,
it worries me.

Is it because I'm thirty-three
and Jesus died at thirty-three
and Nipsey died at thirty-three?

Okay, okay! I'll sign up for it,
why must you hurry me?
I signed up as a prophet,
would that be perjury?
Do you want to murder me?
Inject me!
What's that, third degree?
Excuse me, if I look at this earnestly.
Suddenly, you're concerned with me.
Bending over backwards
serving me,
confusing my firm beliefs
that this was all done purposely.
Either way it's hurting me.
No! I won't watch what I say,
now you search for me.
Mind boggled as I figure out
what works for me…
For life's uncertainty.

FEEL OR FELL

Confusion!
Sometimes I misplace a letter when I write
mixing these two words up,
I noticed an alliance between the two in my life…
A spell casted on me causes me
to unconsciously misspell
So similar they are,
the depressing feeling when I'm down
is just like falling to the ground.
Is it because I fall hard when
I feel for someone
or the disappointment after
a fallout
the rise and fall
of the many different emotions
the tides in the ocean.
I fell in…
"I'm fine!" with getting them mixed up.
Obviously, there's no separating.
And no matter how I relate them
I just hope each time,
I continue to get up.

DREAMS

Hard to explain my nightcaps
I'd rather live in sleep
fear seldomly approaches
as the subconscious smooths the deep

for make believe
or was it clear as day
yesterday's grief
or future's lust

souls' hunger when she visits
enemies can do me no harm
for I run this show
until I snoozed the alarm

then memory erases
the graphic magic
as reality replaces
and I rise to chase my dream

WIND BEFORE THE STORM

Always sends chills,
A cool vibe
that soothes the soul
before the earth cries.

Clouds give a sure sign,
but only if I-
could recognize
the storms in life.

Give me a sure sign,
like a stomach thunder
so I can void-
my own blunder.

No more eye rain,
nice umbrella
for the tempestuous pain-
that leads to the Sun.

DAYS TURN TO NIGHTS, NIGHTS TURN TO
YEARS

Alright! Let's play the waiting game…
Because I sure played the silent game.
Started off, me and my siblings in back
of dads Cadillac, playing the cussing game-
to sticking up the blackjack game.

A hungry man doesn't play no game.
Now public defender runs his game
and they're eating off of my broke back
like they're hunting for game.
Don't song-cry now, it's all part of the game.

I feel like I'm just writing my life away…
Should have I chosen another way?
No daylight or savings, time don't go back.
I wanted to do it my way
so they prided locking me away.

Now my mother done passed away.
An overdose, least she did it her way.
A little late to go back
to the blueprint, somehow-someway
it's time to find a better way.

LOVE IS LOVE (Oowwop)

Thank you for being a brother through the years.
Realized a little too late that only true lovers
and real brothers would be there.
We connect through the hustle and the struggle
where authenticity is a rarity.
I see your love is like mine—charity.
Therefore, greatness is in us, inherently.
And I know we'll shine because
the rock we're cut from,
is of clarity!

SOME STICK IT OUT

I once saw a woman that had a man in prison
had to respect this woman even though this was
forbidden
and she let me scratch that itch
her good heart wouldn't let her leave her man in
prison
with nothing—to come home to nothing
setting him up for failure
you might as well tell him to stay in prison
and spend his life in prison
sad if kids were depending on him
sure, she could have established a decent life with me
but leaving her man in prison for me
would have never sat wright with me
knowing how it feels to be alone
go ahead in the other room and answer the phone…
So, wherever you are,
just know I admire you from afar
like a big loyal star.
Or not.

LET'S LET GO

Forgiveness is forbidden
when resentment is hidden
let's let go,

modesty is love
animosity takes away from love
let's let go,

misery puts
    a dent in me,
        I love you,
            let's let go,

love made the boys and girls
to everything else in this world
the trees and the birds
the voice and the words
let's let go,

It's the only frequency
that speaks to me
I feel it in my soul
the only thing I could
further indulge
let's let go.

RADIOACTIVITY

Damn I love how your freakuency
speaks to me
I'm channeled in
your mind, body and spirit
I could handle them
Sexy—you wear it
radio of love
and I hear it
a ratio, way above-
average,
radioactive-
the way the atoms in our minds radiate and penetrate
transmitting signals from the universe,
filling our bodies with an electrical and chemical
reaction,
no static
on this station
because the world's energy is love and that's
our communication
and how we broadcast it
will be everlasting!

THE OTHER SIDE OF THE SUN

The struggle continues,
will it ever get better,
or are we forever cursed?
Kids don't go to church,
bids or even worse,
take a long, nice ride
in that big black hearse,
the game with no purse,
no fame or no perks,
unless it's Percocets,
provider to all the sets,
jumped off the porch steps,
right into the hellfire,
drug-supplier,
learned his math as he turned 7,
but watch out for your brethren,
on the other side of the weapon,
that sends you back to the essence…

POPCORN

I always liked Carlito.
He just wanted to get out the game.
Is that how it's going to happen for me,
haunted by my past associates and
street fame?
Like on a humbug, unexpected
drop-off with cuz a get you
knocked off.
Just wanted to take his lady to
paradise.
A favor will kill you faster than a
bullet, heard that one twice.
Sometimes we're too loyal to
the ones that don't deserve it.
Like his lawyer played dirty,
he was a real crudball.
Aren't they all?

I liked Benny too.
A little extra but
he wasn't disrespectful.
He should have handled Benny
better.
He just wanted some game and to
be acknowledged by a great.
A big mistake, if you're
gonna' check him, make
sure it's checkmate.
They all gunning for him now.
He moves swift
managing it
wifey waiting
time wasting
and BOOM!

To get set up by his friend.
It's always a friend in the end.
I always liked Carlito.

LAVISH LIED TO ME

King size, with big thighs laid in the A.C.
steak and lobster after you pay me,
rose pedals massaging a pretty lady.

Top down getting topped off
new apartment to a big loft
in class, making drop offs.

Refrigerator full eating takeout
fox scarf around you as we make out.
Bossed! Do what I say now!

I'm flying out, she's flying in!
Life's a gamble, Vegas—I'm buying in
long nights, afternoons lying in.

My gold necklace winnings,
stripes of honor pendant
or is it reckless spending?

Trying to escape the poor me
but pain comes shortly, in order to obtain this glory
but it's all gone by the end of the story…

ANDRE 3000

A Outkast in pissy elevators
watching ceiling fans
go round and round
tryna catch that feeling
from empty refrigerators
and broken air conditions
that's poor conditions
and no more prayers
reached for a snub and
went and found some grub
joyrides in stolen cars
from the back yard
to the prison yard
with your
baby brothers
that turned
into
hustlers

2021

Long way from home
let's not turn on our own.
Some will go as far as
lying on a friend
before they see knights in a pen.
Mass incarceration breaks the heartz of men.
In a round-a-bout,
I am Hectorrrrrr!!
Give my lady an escape route,
knowing I'll never see her again,
still willing to die for my kin.
Pass this honor to my sons,
Brave heart,
young kings on a throne.
Heavy crowns on our sons,
at heart,
we'll never be overthrown.
Streets taught us in reverse,
an inner city curse.
Broken laws tried to make it,
spend it fast or they'll take it.
And no worries about tomorrow,
hurry broke-in sorrow.
Now we have to borrow,
but where are the black banks at?
I know one
it was bombed in Tulsa 1921
that's 100 years
and the smoke still hasn't cleared,
bodies in the sun.
Poverty could be fun,
if you mix it with drugs and alcohol
and the bigger you are
the bigger you will fall.

That's hundred-year sentences
for accused menaces.
Actually he was good overall
but they'll never mention it.

FIGHT

Preliminary

This is the preliminary,
is my humble demeanor more scary?
Am I a successor, from your colonial possession
objective?
No! I won't accept it…
I'm the aggressor, now I'm profiling in possession of
a weapon.
No half-stepping…
Yes oppressor, in denial.
Your profession, a spectrum,
Looking at me flexing.
Now it's my pressure-applied, giving lessons on
protecting
what we have left and…
What we have coming
No more slumming
or succumbing
to your knee-necking.
We rumbling!
Mountains moved, cities crumbling
to rebuild a society so humbling.
No more ugly duckling.
Easy to get stuck in,
this one-way door.
To get out is to endure
a mental beating,
Shut up! Accept defeat and…
tap out on the floor.
But we get up!
We'll never give up!
No touching gloves
or after-hugs.

We will be back for more.

Round 1

This starts off a little ignorant
because in the beginning
we were limited.
Poverty kissed me—Dodd
I'm from where "he died"
probably missed me a dozen times
first time; smuggling dimes
in our behinds
searched by a cop
with frisky hands
first time my heart probably stopped
he swallowed his,
His heart could have popped!
All from our risky plans
these is, nonfictionals
thesis, and we missing bros
why do we make choices
that destroy our lives?
So pitiful and pivotal,
not one who glorifies
and I'm no storier
from where the weak-meek-meet
but by the end of this
you'll see he's a warrior

Round 2

Don't let them ground you
you still slanging
pound for pound
don't let them take you down
hush without a sound

no training
because father's lost
and mother—sauced…
Brother not around
even little sister—gone girl
from the town
we been addicts
no actors
Ben Afflecks
pushed backwards
get up!
6,7,8
off the canvas
equality, pace
chin up straight
God, damage!
Follow me…
Build stamina,
steady, steady, wait…
Now destroy him!

Round 3

Okay, hands up, don't shoot!
Do you know what we go through?
Our provoked youth?
Okay, we'll show you.
One, two, got an understanding
we're not asking we're demanding!
Take our bumps and our bruises
but what's not happening—us losing
and that is proven
no fooling, better schooling
c'mon! What are you doing?
What you thinking,
you're Michael B. Jordan,

a young Adonis?
They don't make it in
our city that often,
but you can find it.
Look what time it is
watch the clock…
Keep your eyes open,
Now find a clean shot!

Round 4

Close them fists
this ain't slapboxing
no training days, Denzels
and Black cops!
When they gave a life sentence
to gram-pops
repentance,
you a fan, stop!
That's where the plan rots
we have to reconstruct
before we self-destruct
or go back to the block
and with our luck
we'll get stuck.
Now you know where that leads
are we that needy
get at mo dog
stop being greedy
bright lights
loud noise
crowd screams
tight fight
bad choice
ears ring
ding! ding! ding!

Round 5

Time to get even
we need a team of them
Shakur Stevensons
out protesting
while we was in the
hole stressing
prison lessons
either wise up
or your vision lessens
hidden message
now you're looking good
get what's owed
hold up, you're getting cold
if you criminal-code
stick to the code
never fold
body shot make him fold
from Essex Co. jail
to running in Africa
rumble in the jungle
or rioting in Attica
if you chose the latter,
now you know I'm mad at ya!

Round 6

We need a win!
Because I've already flunked
it's your time, surpass me
I like them trunks
materialistic stigmas
we must get rid of
what could I say
we like nice things

we come from the mud
that's where we played
for that belt and them rings
but what we needed was love
no trophy is going to show me
or shut me up!
You better knock me out!
Bloody nose—stuff me up
or eye-cut me up...
Blind me with diamonds
when we the ones that find them
in the first place—the birthplace
just give me some water
my son and my daughters
and a couple books to read
and I promise you I won't falter

Round 7

Babygirl,
you ready for this cruel world?
I know you could handle it
but we have to dismantle it
I'm a step in
fathers protect them
let no one disrespect them
sick and tired of misdirection
and federal correction
What are you doing standing out here?
I'm starving bro.
No! Go home with your daughter bro
that father-daughter connection
that's what we invest in!
Them young hearts of gold!

WHERE DO LITTLE SOULS GO?

Guess you had enough.
Her Sun shines.
The sun dries the eyes,
on a windy day.
I looked to the sky,
the top of the trees
swayed back
and forth,
waving
goodbye.
"There she goes." I smiled.
The leaves celebrate.
We mourned since
we were born.
Devastating,
passes the storm
when we die
pain no more.
I see you baby
dressed in linen
high off the fly!
Maybe one day
together again,
we'll go
swimming
in the sky.

MOURN WITH ME

The tears wouldn't make an exit
but they'll well up
though we all would like to make an exit
while we're well up

but the scars are the stars
that makes us light up
for love

find the gentleness in the hard
until the fights up
fight for love

LIKE A QUEEN BEE

If I ruled the world…
I would lead with love
in search for peace
that's just me…
But in reality,
I would have to add
some equality
in defense because
evidently
things can get bad.
And naturally I'll sting.

Or shall I be prone to abuse?
Depicting one's good motives
from one's wickedness is like
playing duck-duck-goose.
But what you'll do or whom
you will allow in your life,
is all on how you choose.
Unless choice is— exploited.

We won't let the ills of the
world take away from our truth,
and never let it change the
good in you.
We only stay aware
so we can be wise with our care
as we prepare
to strengthen love—
everywhere…

RELEASE PLAN

Just give me a hoody and a thermal set
for the hoods thermostat.

Cold heart
cold days
in a cold world.

Remember we would wear face masks
all winter, easier to disguise the sinner.
Didn't know it protected us from germs.
Pints of alcohol with no flask,
is how we cleaned the germs
and our wounds.
For the beginner,
first sip usually burns.
Drunk, putting babies in wombs
selfishly without a care—
if they're deemed for doom,
see you soon…
Now my first investment- a book!
My new weapon, shoot you in the head
for protection.
Who knew that's all it took?
Guided and decided on misdirection.
Learning, if you take away the L, makes an earning,
happiness, passion and success.
Common sense proved this,
guess we were senseless,
the uncommon young and ruthless.
Creepin on a come up.

The To Do List

-Relax and watch the sun come up

-Bad back—get good health insurance
-Bag packed, for the world we're exploring
-Reach back,
to the prisons for the other siblings
-Only take a kneel
to ask my kids for forgiveness

When he spilled
and explained, you could hear the pain.
Other than that, you wouldn't know it.
For his campaign,
Would never show it.

LET ME FLY

Clouds flew past
as the sun laughed,
slow down, where to so fast?

Normality is abnormal
when caged so long,
Wow freedom!' I sighed.

Singing an informal,
'So long!
Now let me fly…

ABOUT THE AUTHOR

Born in Newark, NJ, Mario F Wright grew up in the neighboring city of East Orange where he quickly found the struggles of life and made choices that led him into trouble. Formerly incarcerated, Wright's life takes a different direction with his aim focused on sharing his experiences to help others. He performs his poetry under the name Influential Finesse as he places his influence on people sharing his finesse with the world. Wright is a leader in his community with three marvelous children and he presently lives in New York City.